BROKEN ·DAWN
BLESSINGS

ADAM SOL

POEMS

BROKEN DAWN
BLESSINGS

Published by ECW Press
665 Gerrard Street East
Toronto, Ontario, Canada M4M 1Y2
416-694-3348 / info@ecwpress.com

Editor for the Press: Michael Holmes/
a misFit book
Cover design: Rachel Ironstone
Cover image: © iStock / stanley45
Author photo: Mark Raynes Roberts

LIBRARY AND ARCHIVES CANADA CATALOGUING IN
PUBLICATION

Title: Broken dawn blessings : poems / Adam Sol.

Names: Sol, Adam, 1969- author.

Identifiers: Canadiana (print) 20210209186 |
Canadiana (ebook) 20210209208

ISBN 978-1-77041-606-2 (softcover)
ISBN 978-1-77305-818-4 (ePub)
ISBN 978-1-77305-819-1 (PDF)
ISBN 978-1-77305-820-7 (Kindle)

Classification: LCC PS8587.O41815 B76 2021 | DDC
C811/.6—dc23

We acknowledge the support of the Canada Council for the Arts. *Nous remercions le Conseil des arts du Canada de son soutien.*
This book is funded in part by the Government of Canada. *Ce livre est financé en partie par le gouvernement du Canada.* We
acknowledge the support of the Ontario Arts Council (OAC), an agency of the Government of Ontario, which last year
funded 1,965 individual artists and 1,152 organizations in 197 communities across Ontario for a total of $51.9 million. We also
acknowledge the support of the Government of Ontario through the Ontario Book Publishing Tax Credit, and through
Ontario Creates.

 ONTARIO
CREATES

 ONTARIO ARTS COUNCIL
CONSEIL DES ARTS DE L'ONTARIO
an Ontario government agency
un organisme du gouvernement de l'Ontario

Canada Council   Conseil des arts
for the Arts   du Canada

 Canadä

PRINTED AND BOUND IN CANADA   PRINTING: COACH HOUSE   5 4 3 2 1

Table of Contents

These poems follow a trajectory that is roughly parallel
to the *Birkhot HaShachar* (Blessings of the Dawn),
a series of prayers recited by observant Jews
immediately upon waking each morning.

Waiting

מי שברך אבותינו מקור הברכה לאמותנו...

It's 8 am, she just went in, which I guess means the anesthesiologist is holding her hand, looking for a vein. I met him before I said goodbye, he said *No trouble* a lot while she asked her nervous questions. Five times in the five minutes we had with him before they shooed me away. He hadn't shaved. How many of these does he do in a day?

There were two women in the holding area getting ready to go in, Y and an older white-haired lady whose husband had a look on his face like he was angry about the whole thing. Or maybe he was trying to keep from crying. We all have reason to be angry, though at what or whom I can't say. At cancer, I guess. But how is a man supposed to express his anger at a thing that grows inside his wife? Even if it wants to eat her.

The attending nurse points me down the hall. I'm wearing her hair tie like a ring on my finger. Carrying her purse in my fist. The corridor walls are pasty green and the floors are that forgiving material that can be soiled and cleaned and soiled and cleaned forever, and will never look more or less than dingy. There's the sign on a door, Family Waiting Room, but it's locked, so what can I do, I sit on the floor and play FreeCell on my phone. Something I can put into order. Echoing footsteps from around corners like an old elementary school. The janitors and nurses and consultants keep passing by, and everyone says they'll call the security guy to open up. They're all giving me that same raised-eyebrow sympathy I've been fending off for weeks since the diagnosis, but at least here there's something concrete they can do. Open the fucking door.

It's 8:30 which means I guess she's under by now, and the marks that they made on her chest with markers are starting to look like a map to the ones who can read it.

Packing a bag last night, Y insisted I bring lots of snacks, as if I were going on some trip. The hospital is downtown, there's a food court downstairs and fifty restaurants within a two-block radius. Maybe after all the talk about nausea she wanted to make sure that one of us was eating. So I packed grapes and crackers, cheese and chocolate, now all scattered in my bag and crumbling into each other while I dig around, looking for a pen.

The security guard, all apologetic, comes around the corner in a bulletproof vest and lets me into the room. Windowless, fluorescent lighting, with pamphlet displays and magazines on the Formica tables and a few packets of cookies. At least I can put everything down. No tv and the wifi spotty, so I don't have to keep track of the latest chaos.

It's 9, which means I guess they've cut her open and are extracting and probing. There are her muscles, and her veins and her fat and her bones exposed to the air for the first time in her life, and the microbes expelled from the lungs of the nurses, and the bacteria remaining from last night's procedures all swimming around the room, and probably a bit of her blood on the blue napkins they use, and the attendants and who the hell else is in there looking on, residents and orderlies and fellows and then the great surgeon himself, the Maestro, the one we pulled strings to secure, with his bushy blond eyebrows, everyone looking inside the body of my wife, who lies there breathing through a tube, a human being in suspension.

There's a couple arrived here in the Family Waiting Room whose teenaged daughter just got sent in for surgery. They're talking about Ronald McDonald House and being able to afford the renos they'll have to do on their place — leukemia, a bone marrow transplant. They look ugly and tired, wearing ridiculous sweaters and talking too loudly, and I can't help them while they try to understand how their iPhones work.

Saying goodbye to the sleepy kids at dawn while her visiting sister made their school lunches. Middle boy hugged her and said, "Do a good job, Mom." She said, "It's the doctor who has to do a good job. I just have to lay there."

There are so many pamphlets in here, it's as if we're in a rest area at a tourist trap. Try the Railway Museum. Take a course in Coping with Cancer. Nutritional Seminars. Apple Picking. Look Great, Feel Better.

9:20 went to get coffee on the lobby level and saw the Hs waiting on his blood work. They're here every week. Inoperable brain tumour. She had breast cancer a few years ago. Makes you wonder what's in the water. Then he lost his father. How much pain and suffering can be delivered upon one family? His speech is halting and his cheeks have expanded, but he still has a good crinkled smile and she sounds outrageously upbeat. Medication? She wants to give me advice, but I want to get back to the Waiting Room so that I can do the thing I'm supposed to do. At some point the Maestro is supposed to come in and give me an update. If I'm not there when he arrives I won't find out if she's got six months to recover or six months to live.

Her heart. The question of how her heart will handle the strain and confusion. Her enormous, faithful, graceful heart. Feeling, for the first time, a draft through the chest wall.

It's 10 am now, which means I guess that they're halfway through, they're waiting on the rapid pathology report of her sentinel nodes so that they can decide whether or not to yank into her arm and perform an axillary lymphectomy. That would mean the cancer has spread and I'm not ready to think about what else. The hallways here are full of people who are waiting on this sort of news. Mammograms and blood work, and biopsies and CT scans. If you are clear, you leave and you come back as infrequently as possible. If you are not, you move to a different corridor and start on other kinds of work, with other kinds of consequences, words, and worries.

10:20 maybe the Reconstructionist is beginning his work now on the first side while the surgeon pulls apart the other. Implanting the expanders like little saline balloons that are going to give her back her shape and pride once this mess is over with, and have been the main source of our humour pre-surgery. *I won't be able to keep my hands off them! Fine with me, I won't feel it.*

The end of the exquisite delight of feeling her nipples clench under my touch. The end of that forever.

10:35 and suddenly the Maestro is at the doorway of the waiting room, his eyebrows the only expressive part of him. He massages his neck and says, laconically, "Things went well: her nodes tested negative." And then he's off to wash his hands, grab a coffee, and cut into someone else. He's not even halfway through his day. And I'm sitting in the Family Waiting Room, trying to comprehend his one sentence.

11:05 I've texted the family and there's a collective electronic sigh of relief battering around our email accounts and cellphones that expresses itself in all caps and multiple exclamation points as if it is almost over already when in fact we're just through part one of stage one and at least there's something I've done for the past half hour while I've been waiting. Because the book in my lap is still on the same page it was on when I sat down.

11:45 means she's in recovery, the desk nurse said I just have to wait outside until the ward nurse is ready to wheel her up to her room. All these different types of nurses who have their different attitudes and approaches, and it's hard to tell if this one is clipped and formal because that's the prescribed attitude of "desk nurse," or if she's just a clipped and formal person. Knowing I'll find out more about this in the next twenty-four hours than I'd known before. The nurses in the maternity ward when our boys were born were universally smiley, who wouldn't be? But even there, there were some who were matter-of-fact and businesslike when helping her breastfeed or checking the baby's temp, and some who looked like they wanted to come home with us to stay while we settled in and we probably would have let them if we could.

11:50. I've spent the last five minutes standing in the hall, watching my phone count seconds backwards. Or maybe that was a stopwatch function.

12:05. They wheel her out backwards, the nurse is impatient, she doesn't want to miss the elevator to the recovery ward, wait, *wait*. I can see the top of her hair all askew — didn't they put it in one of those showercaps during the surgery? The nurse is nasty and pulls the bed into the elevator, starts talking to an orderly with a rack full of gowns. He shoves it aside and she pushes my wife against the wall.

We have been married nineteen years. She has never looked more vulnerable, more ghostly, ethereal, and yet also fleshy, a person in her body which has been altered and redefined. The gown is hanging off her and her shape is collapsed into the bed and she's confused and her hair is everywhere eyes closing and opening wanting water but she hears me when I say her nodes tested negative and she cries a little and then we're in the elevator listening to the nasty nurse talk about how she's going on vacation tomorrow and she can't wait to get out of town she can't wait to feel the humid heat again and I don't care I don't care you go away while I turn to cradle her head awkwardly in my arm trying to hold all our everything together.

On First Waking

מודה אני לפניך...

after alarm
before insistent Monday sun

after restless sleep in a bed basted in pain
before reused coffee grounds cold shower torn screen

after the answer yes again these bones
before the stench really settles

after the riots and crackdowns
before the crackdowns and riots

after patrols rumble through the neighbourhood for a final sweep
before wonder becomes worry and worry wrangles its way back to
    work

after the return of my mind to my eyes
before the mirror reminds me of my face smearing to mustard

after the knowledge that rising will be painful
before the sensation

in the blur between
motion and stillness

blessing and complaint

I acknowledge you my joints
faithful to your faults

return my sore soul to me

the new day the old day
the burden of being the halter

Ducts and Conduits

‎…נקבים נקבים, חלולים חלולים.

Monday morning,
bitter sunrise,
sirens from the east.

My city
has convinced itself
that one type of strife

is insufficient,
so it is grafting.
But dawn still

calm enough
for ritual —
the mug, the porch,

a glutted skunk
trudges home.
Twenty minutes

between making lunches
and waking Y for her meds.
Hard as it is

to believe in anything
I believe in bus
lines, power lines,

yellow lines in the road
we all know
how to use.

Thanks for the sewers
working still
as far as I know

and the water
purification plant
wherever it is.

If even one
of our network of valves
and passageways failed

the whole shebang
would go shebang.
Oh there it is now

the first pillar
of smoke and the day
officially underway.

Old Faker, Fraud,
when can I see You?
What would I say?

Immerse

לעסוק בדברי תורה...

Upstairs my wife is sleeping off
    her incisions

while I butter bread for our boys
    and anticipate

the battered sedan that rifles Monday's
    Star at my stoop

my tea is hot but weak and for twenty
    minutes I will

soak in yesterday's analysis already
    too late

no account of the violence that bloomed
    overnight

while this paper was being printed
    my city pulps

so I grab a cereal box and read
    the side panels

I will immerse in the word
    for its own sake

until the crying begins in my house
    and everywhere else

Blessing for Twitter

דיין האמת. ...

Before I am fully a person
    I want to know what great
horror happened in the night.
    The icon's head
is too thick for its hopeful wings
    but responds to my thumb
like a faithful servant of the Eternal.
    Give me insult and dogs,
give me West Coast results
    and a drunk self-own from B at 3 am.
Give me the stream of those I admire
    who have been fighting all night
for truth, and the maniacs who hate
    everything they can't touch.
Concentrate, NIMBY. Today, do
    some work that is not
fuelled by rage. But first,
    do some work with rage.
Just outside, a robin cackles
    its first bad joke of the day.
Grey unruly dawn begins
    to interfere with the clear
loud light in my palm.

Reward without Measure

אלו דברים שאין להם שיעור...

Y's surgery was a success
    but the year will still suck.

The prescription: slash, poison,
    and burn. The complete

three-course cancer meal. For now,
    pain, nausea,

and her body trying to understand
    its predicament.

Later I'll speak brightly to her parents
    and maybe bring

a bottle to welcome our new Mexican
    neighbours.

There are groceries to order,
    a newlywed cousin

to send warm wishes to.
    This afternoon,

I won't sneak away to help bury the boy
    who turned his back

when he should have raised his hands.
    There are wounds to tend,

hair to brush, and I might dream
a brief dream

about her healthy body
while staring out

at the smoke up the road. Buster,
you have truly

fucked us up this time. She is my Y,
there is no other.

How can You expect me to make a list
of holy obligations

with my throat closed in worry? Now
it's Your turn

to show me how to break the dawn
into blessing.

The Soul You Have Given Me

אלוהי נשמה שנתת בי...

The good widow keeps
            inviting me
        to play online Scrabble

but I can't bring myself
            to let her win.
        My life is littered

with missed chances to do
            better in the world.
        The sum of these impulses

often ignored or late
            in myself and my
        neighbours is what

God is. That's who
            I pray to.
        Whom.

"Whom" worth twelve points
            even without
        the double word score.

Restores the Dead

...המחזיר נשמות לפגרים מתים.

Blessings upon the earth-
worm descended from
hermaphrodite stowaways
aboard eighteenth-century
Dutch tulip imports
and speared here
in my yard by a jaunty
juvie American robin.
Pedigree won't save your life.
But your sugars and proteins,
exhilarating the speckled
breast of the bird,
will transcend the earth
and mark the separation
between dawn and morning
when the hotshot crows
his way to a perch
on the electric wires.

Gives the Rooster Understanding

‎...אשר נתן לשכוי בינה להבחין בין יום ובין לילה.

Have to keep the tv sound
        down to eggshell
    Y's fragile sleep

It's all police shootings anyway
        police shooting news
    police shooting movies

even police shootings in sports
        so I go out to the porch
    where an idiotic robin

built her nest too close to my chair
        now she's scared to feed
    her chicks while I'm sitting here

Another bloody summer
        halfway finished
    and not a soul among us

who can set the broken bone
        of the world aright
    Okay here she tries again

another angle from the awning
        Come redneck
    come at me in my seeing seat

I am here with my cracked mug
of wakefulness
desperate to believe

The Little President

שנתן מכבודו לבשר ודם. ...

When I go out at sunrise
to dispose of our waste
there is a small President
in the middle of the road
he must have fallen
from the nest not yet
ready for prime time
his suit is mostly formed
still patches of baby fuzz
I don't know if he hurt
himself or is just stunned
by his campaign failure
when I first approach
he looks up and opens
his beak expecting food
or applause not yet
aware of the danger he is in
exposed to passing traffic
above in the maple
his campaign manager
is urging action
offering encouragement
so I don some garden gloves
and escort the President
to the green fringe
where he'll be safe
to regroup his resources
he's not happy being handled
and tries to flop away

from my personal touch
his staff swoops overhead
unsure if I mean him harm
I say Don't worry Little
President and set him down
gently so he can waddle
under the burdock
where I leave him to be
cared for by those who
know him best while I go
inside to make oatmeal
for my own hatchlings
all day we can hear
the President bleat
a steady series of requests
for his staff who descend
to offer morsels
some of which he consumes
but we all can see
it won't be enough
our efforts and good
wishes within days
he'll lose popular support
and be left alone
to shiver alongside
the sprinkler head
if there weren't so many
Presidents populating
our neighbourhood
my boys and I might
feel compelled
to shoebox him and apply
more drastic measures
but who's to say

our volunteer hours
would produce measurable
results soon enough
the yellow jackets
will devour him
feathers flesh and slogan
feathers song and bone

Elegy for a Youth Shot by Police on the Day Robin Williams Died

August 11 circles round again
    and a new doc appears to celebrate
        Robin Williams's life and artistry.
While Spirits and the Muse illuminate
    the web with clips from standup, interviews,
        random hilarity shared with the gaffers and crew

(concealing pain we should have recognized),
    there is a corner of the internet
        dedicated to your memory:
your sister posted an In Memoriam page;
    the funeral home offers public space
        under your obituary for

heartfelt testimonials; there's also
    a dormant but unpurgèd Instagram
        account that once you made more lovely
with selfies in flat cap, graduation gown.
    Someone could Google your common name and find
        your profile in the *Picayune* before

the paywall shuts her out. Of course complete
    transcripts from the failed investigation
        are in the public record, held in storage
in the white radiance of a server housed
    somewhere in Oklahoma City. Have you
        seen his warm exchange with soldiers serving

in Kuwait? How many young men died that day?
    Half the jokes in *Good Morning Vietnam*
        were ad-libbed for the camera crew. No doubt

he was the Sire of an Immortal Strain.
    And that was *after* he kicked cocaine, "God's way
        of saying you have too much fucking money."

What hard mishap hath doomed this blameless swain?
    Apparently you kept your hands concealed
        during an investigative stop
for thirteen seconds from the moment when
    the felon winds appointed you their next
        and the bullets that would now themselves disown.

It must be said his Boston accent was
    not convincing. But the performance?
        Transcendent nonetheless, although some say
his first success as a moving tragic clown
    was in *Seize the Day*, dir. Fielder Cook.
        You bled out from the misty dream of life,

choking your last in an asphalt parking lot,
    wasting your sweetness on the desert air
        while the blush on your chest expanded wide to take
in the fresh paint, the dim streetlights, even
    the Gang Squad panting in their body armour.
        A heart once pregnant with celestial fire

now blown apart by superior ballistics.
    We will not be distracted. We will not be
        dismissive of depression and its toll.
Let passion-wingèd Ministers of Thought
    forge memes and PSAs to keep us focused.
        Grief is mortal, the internet is not.

We are all guilty for his death because
    "we wanted more of him than he could give."

Let talk about depression now increase
with its new famous patron saint and martyr.
Let all accept responsibility
for our sins of omission on August 11.

Let this day forever serve to remind us
of those we could have saved, laurelled or
dishonoured, friend and foe alike. Let no
more life divide what Death can join together.
Sleep with comedians and kings, clear Sprites.
Tomorrow to fresh pastimes and headlines new.

Who Made Me a Jew

‏...שֶׁעָשַׂנִי יִשְׂרָאֵל.

If I were anything more
    than an old sock
I would know how to bless
    without a but

but I am a Jew on a Wednesday
    morning and look
at my city splintering

kids who would prefer
    to bash mailboxes
have to decide how to respond
    to militarized law enforcement

pull down hoodies
    Instagram the consequences

at least I am a Jew
    I can say we know
about the riptide turning

    hey look we invented
shame-in-your-nation

the radio wakes up
with a blast of warning
        traffic and a gunman
both slowing the commute
        my Y in our room

sitting up for some orange juice

Emptying the Drains

‫...שֶׁלֹּא עָשַׂנִי אִשָּׁה.‬

The receptacles hang from her sides,
odd ornaments or

bulbs from a baster, attached
by elastic tubes

that siphon lymph and blood
from wounds

that used to be her breasts.
Careful now.

She can't raise her arms so it's tough
to do alone though

some women must. *Careful.* Pinch
near her rib

and draw down
to milk the liquid,

thick red from the first days
now washing

out closer to clear. A warm iron
smell still rich

in the bathroom. Sneak a peak
at the yanked

scar on her *careful* sharp wince
if the tug

is too severe. 4 ml is down
from yesterday

and good, no sign of infection. Measure
then rinse

the egg vessels, gently settle
the baubles back

into place at her sides. We will never speak
of the intimacies

of these weeks, she won't meet
my eye while

I ease the nightshirt back over her head
and walk her back

to the procedural she's bingeing on.

Not a Slave

שֶׁלֹּא עָשַׂנִי עֶבֶד...

A squirrel trapped in my trash
    hurls himself at the lid.
All that frantic pain over
    an old rind of brie like me,
the paunch on the porch
    with a cupful of steam
who can take a week
    to care for his wife
while she recovers from surgery.
    Don't take that lightly,
don't take those blessings lightly,
    the boys who can
walk themselves to school, neighbours
    I can call when I need
to run away for a few hours,
    the house that stands
over us in its bulky embrace.
    I'll be the dope
who tips the bin to set the beast free,
    trailing a muck
of mouldy bread and mustard.

Lacunal

— for Harold Heft

We were once ambitious
and conflicted. We had
projects in mind. I
remember an anguished
argument over Woody
Allen's sins. While hoisting
baby boys into bumper
cars we made sweeping
judgments and plans. But
now the tumour has made
off with the strength
of your right hand and
a fifth of your prodigious
vocabulary. So I pour
the milk and supply
the odd abstract noun.
Meanwhile your tone is so
upbeat I can't decide
if it's mortal bliss
or mood alteration.
We briefly discuss a book
you'll never finish and finally
your wife returns
from her hour of frantic
errands to escort you away.
Through the café window
I watch her tuck an arm
under your elbow as you
wait, perfectly composed,
for the light to change.

Public Expression

Why all this weeping?
I heard about the earthquake in Nepal

but that's hardly urgent enough for the torrents
I'm witnessing at the SuperJuice.

What has befallen us?
What stream must I tap to discover the worst?

It must be here somewhere.
Send me the link and I'll share.

I can grieve with the most circumspect
of our public broadcasters but so far all I see

are the last throes of a Sumatran species
and an arson in Tonawanda.

Search "disaster" and find everything.
And yet the citizens here are tearing their hair.

Some have even shut their laptops
to whimper at the windows. Are they further

in the know? I see the market is crashing but
that's just a continuation from last week.

Would the aftershocks cause such a convulsion
when we've lost so much already?

I hear no ambulance. The cop on the corner,
in his riot gear and assault rifle,

seems calm and poised behind his visor —
no wait, his shoulders also shake.

His gun points distractedly at his partner.
Has someone holy been martyred? The servers

and blenders are too busy for news
but even they seem aware of the crisis.

What has happened?
For whom shall I mourn?

Neither Are You Free to Desist

‏...לא אתה בן חורין ליבטל ממנה.‏

There's another version of myself
    who takes to the street

to sing songs and throw stones
    at what's rotten in my city

He leaves off nursing and spends
    less time on his own porch

He has sabotage in mind
    He has already burned bridges

I admire him
    this man who acts

who takes a beating in the service of
    who speaks in a big gathering voice

I admire him
    but before Y wakes

I must ensure this ant
    exploring the banister

has made it safely to the garden
    Let's not kid ourselves

I am in most ways a complacent coward
    See how the creature

realigns its antenna before setting off again
    back towards my porch

Hey Bossman
    why does it know where to go?

(Going to) Where It's Happening

My friends at the bureau
told me, "If you go there,
bring a pistol." So I
bought one at a show
and hid it with my teeth.

The streets were bloated
with people whose language
I barely understood
though they were my countrymen,
citizens like myself

who had gone further
with rage than I could,
even in my imagination.
They had set fires.
They had torn bolts away

from metal panels I thought
couldn't be bent. Some at
the sandwich shop couldn't pay,
others only had foreign currency,
but the harried owner fed

them all, even the under
cover, even the unborn.
There were explosive sounds
coming from the central square
and as I picked my way

along came a green-eyed man
in a tailored shirt
bleeding from the temple.
He shouted at the helicopters
then seized my arm, pleading

in rapid-fire argot
that I should repent or repeat
his story but frankly
all that cohered for me
was his blood, which by then

had streamed down his arm
onto the fingers that seized
my sleeve. I do not know
which side of things he found
himself bleeding for,

whether I agreed with him,
or what he really wanted done.
I did what I could: I mopped
his cheek with newspaper, I made
sympathetic noises. I gave him the gun.

According to Your Will

שעשני כרצונו*...*

Thursday morning calm against all sense
    while Y winces in her sleep

and my city turns concrete action
    into abstract lies.

I feel the pull of bad news from the screen
    but there's plenty here:

raccoons have disembowelled the feeder,
    and up above

a hawk has discovered the cardinals' nest
    and is feasting on the chicks

while the parents harass and screech.

I hear you darlings but cannot help,
    you have no appreciation

for the larger forces at work, the trends
    and legalities.

I want to be good. I want to be
    seen to be good.

But I am also only as I was made.

What I do is offer blessing
    on behalf of my Y

while she occupies herself
    with more urgent work.

It would have been preferable

עכשיו שנברא...

This project
    these poems you are reading

She'd rather not be part of it
    She'd rather we both respect her privacy

These poems
    like her cancer
        something between us

Or to write from my porch
    about the pain in my city
        the violence down the hill

After thirty months of debate
    the Rabbis' conclusion is

it would have been better
    if humanity had never been created

however now that it's too late to alter

we should examine our actions
    with probing hands

No we should scrutinize and evaluate
    so we can improve

They contend carefully over the verbs

Opens the Eyes

פוקח עוורים. ...

Thursday morning
    cracked back
and the humidity
    tightening
from the dollar
    store straight
to my forlorn
    corner of this
spent earth.
    Everywhere
I see incompleteness.
    Will You scatter
or fulfill?
    Is there anywhere
we can go to find You?
    Is there better
reception
    at the community
centre? No I must
    seek You here,
at Eglinton and Kiss
    My Ass,
the Mastectomy section.
    Here let me hunt
Your Un-ness.
    Brick houses
are stumpy and sullen
    and the windows

sealed shut. But
  we will
not remain uncalled.
  We will
be summoned. Even
  now I invent
a signal for You to wire out
  across the nations.
Don't You dare forsake me,
  after all
this bullshit. You *will* call to me,
  to all of us
slurping through our first cup
  before dawn.
I double-dog dare You to be what
  I hope You are.

Clothes the Naked

‎...מלביש ערומים.

With the fog and the damp
　　it's going to be hard
to set myself on fire.

Already boys in their Teflon onesies
　　are ready to tear
the world apart to see

Your justice on earth.
　　Why must we wait?
If the sum total

of all these actions, the patterns
　　and reflexes,
kindnesses and counting,

if all this cannot bring about
　　the deluge
I'm going to have to

throw my bones on the pile.
　　Someone's started
breakfast — I can smell

the sizzle. But this old bowling
　　jersey will hold
until the burning begins.

Butcher

שהכל נהיה בדברו. ...

Trinkets of muscle, flesh from empathetic
creatures, lounge on plates and slabs
over a frozen mattress, the barrel-shaped
ice pebbles reaching out with their steam
to embrace the corpses, the steaks,
the severed sections of cow. What I mean is
even the vapour in the refrigerated cabinet
understands something has been lost
but that won't stop it from surrounding
everything it can with effervescence
as if it might encourage the meat lying there,
marbled and lean, boned and marinated,
shorn from the carcass of a massive beast
or perhaps from a series of beasts, siblings,
sisters, standing together under our fluorescent
attention the way the animals when alive
might have stood together, heads alert,
to watch a passing bus on the highway
near their farm, a place where they've
always felt safe and so the looking, the raised
heads and watchful ears are not alarmed,
hardly even curious, but rather just open
to the new stimulus, the unfamiliar sound
puncturing and then transcending their usual focus
on the grass below their hooves now pickled
in bottles at the far end of the counter where
my fragile sons, elbowing each others' ribs,
wait for me to choose our evening meal.

Frees the Captive

‏...מתיר אסורים.

A gypsy moth flutters my cup
of reconstituted orange drink.

Last night a raccoon was flattened
by a patrolling armoured personnel carrier.
One of us is going to have to spatula
the carcass into a dumpster
that isn't burning.

The scan revealed
only that she has
a long repair horizon.

It's true the lyric is merely
an instrument of escape —
like a shiv filed
from a plastic spork.

On my deaf neighbour's land,
the cubs are screaming in a tree.

Frees the Captive, Again

‏...מתיר אסורים.‏

Raccoon scat
    and skunk funk
basketball hoop
    lowered so
the boys can dunk
    This morning
there is care
    and cooperation
among sparrows
    who don't want
to alert the squirrels
    that the feeder
has been refilled

First human sound
    is sirens south
and a crash that
    could be construction
What have you
    in storage, Absent
Manager? Which version
    of the flood
have you uploaded
    into the system?
Where can my boys
    my Y and I
find the tools to build
    whatever absurd
contraption might save us?

It may be

too late

to complete

the vessel

that might

save you

anyhow

set the saw

to the wet

wood or

are you saying

you will be

one born

in a flood time

who did

not strive to

build boats?

Whale Fall Suspension

They can create complex localized ecosystems
that supply sustenance to deep-sea organisms for decades.
— Hermanus Online, *June 2016*

The downpour of carcasses slowed, then stopped.
It must be the fault of some sin we committed.
What did we do? And how to repent?
Where to find insight and nourishment now
if not from the gifts that have always descended?
Heaven is empty.
The light above, always tempting
for those who are prone to such feelings, now beckoned.
The bravest among us formed expeditions
to explore and, if possible, conquer. But none
returned. Our scientists insist
the atmosphere is toxic. Our sages
swear there are monsters too evil for dreams.
The higher planes are not to be explained.
So we burrow deeper and pray for change.

Lifts Up the Fallen

זוקף כפופים.‏

There's alcohol and aspartame,
microparticles trying to kill us.
Sugar and gluten. Men in the road with machetes.
CSIS, ISIS, Vicodin, crisis. Headscarves
with mysterious codings stitched into the weave.
Gas and uranium, glaciers calving,
seas rising — we are fucked,
even if San Antonio can win
with just the right kind of game.
Don't even start with your helpful alternatives.
Just hold this anvil while I scramble
up the muddy bank to where the fence
has gapped enough to breach.

Spreads the Land over the Water

רוקע הארץ על המים...

Y up and about, padding from bed
    to chair, novel to Netflix.
        She asks me to help

tie back her hair, then stop hovering.
    Friday storm approaches.
        A pulse in the yard dirt,

midges scramble for safety
    under the burdock,
        and down the green hill

another man's son is
    gunned down before his eyes.
        So says the radio.

Once I was afraid to shout and now
    I face the consequences
        of that fear.

The vaults of the righteous are sealed,
    guarded by terrified thirtysomethings
        in full Kevlar.

Which obligations must I fulfill to guarantee
    a peaceful night in my aching
        city? Who knows

that secret? Only You, who won't say
        a damned thing. Now here
                it comes at last,

thick blobs of sweat from uptown
        infused with petrochemicals.
                Seeker, Mute Sentinel,

bring forth the downpour. The weeds will
        know what to make of it.
                Rinse the earth, Uncle.

Then build us back into something
        that won't shame our descendants.

Last Summer at the Beach

שעשה את הים הגדול...

A swarm of fingerlings careens along the surface
near our hips as we bob over the waves, so calm
this morning the boys complain. I'm cold
but I'm the first uncle available so I duck
my head and try to remember how it felt
to be in a body so young and unspoilt, the oiliness
of mother-applied sunscreen sheening my shoulders.
The fish inevitably attract the terns
who face flop in their black visors
and can somehow sing triumph with a full mouth.
The terns bring the gulls who bully their way in
and make a big mess. What the fuck, man.
Over in the shallows some introverted crabs
display their scars to any who'd dare disturb them,
even the pipers tap-dancing the waterline
for edible morsels of dust. What is it like in that carapace?
Now a three-hundred-pound giant struggles
to the water, a vertical scar between his navel
and beltline. Once in, he dives with ease
and even a measure of grace. It's still too early
for the bombastic boogie boarders to claim
territory for their runways. Families are just now
arriving with their barrels and coolers.
The town lifeguards are huddled in their hoodies.
A trio of sun-leathered duchesses
march past with their elbows swinging. Since her stroke,
K needs fifteen minutes to cross the sunparched walkway
over the sawgrass. Now she settles into a chair
and trains her vigilant gaze at her daughter
leaping into the surf after a flying disc.

Provides for My Needs

שעשה לי כל צרכי...

I wanted to start the day with praise
　　but when the garbage truck
　　　　took a look at the debris
　　and turned away again
I summoned a curse in my throat

and hauled my bin, my receipts and rinds,
　　half a mile on a broken wheel
　　　　to the open dumpsters
　　at the Jiffy Lube and added
my offering to the soiled filters and empty

tubs of lubricant. On the way home now,
　　bouncing the can on our cracked
　　　　walkways, allow me,
　　Wayward Manager, to bless
the refuse of my resourceful people.

See how we will tunnel our traces
　　into the roots of the world.

Makes Firm Our Steps

...הַמֵּכִין מִצְעֲדֵי גָבֶר.

Tear gas is a finely tuned instrument
    of municipal administration.

Keep your bleeding eyes on file.

I walk the new stray over chunks of broken
    concrete into a hiss of refusals
        and recording devices.

The boy with headphones larger than his head
    bobs his weave to his own —

Run from the police run from the police

Here they come, billboards on display.
    Who will oppose them?

I will.
With my Shih Tzu, a crap baggie,
    and a ring of keys.

"You Reach the Conclusions"

Poems are all pain
protest or praise
sometimes hard
to tell which

Me I make
praise poems that
sound like protest

Then I fret
about my privilege
which is boring
and not helpful

I confuse to-do lists
with drafts
which is fine

Everyone on the bus
keeps checking their phones
and hating the world

I can tell by the
mouth movements
which bad news
they are scrolling

If they confirm
that scumbag of
course they'll
confirm him

Someone pulls a string
and the bus bumbles
to the curb so
at least that works

A woman can still
pull some strings around here
and stop the ride
so she can get off

She hoists purse
pleather laptop case
three grocery bags
and a kid's backpack

From my seat I watch
her shake out a cherry red
umbrella she conjured
from some invisible pocket

Then with a shoulder lift
that shifts the whole earth
she gets her bearings
and heads south

As we pull away
the man next to me
tells his friend

about the spirit
of his dead lover
appearing to him
in the form of sunshine

Manifesto

שהחיינו וקיימנו והגיענו לזמן הזה. ...

Long before the maintenance men
        came to sweep us away
    with their battered brooms and bromides,

long before the wily commentators conspired
        to water us down
    with taglines and balanced reporting,

long before the governor gave permission
        to his merry ministers
    to have their way with the remainders,

we had come to understand that our representatives
        were holding us lightly
    in abeyance or contempt

and that nothing was beneath them,
        and so we'd need
    to rally our arguments and stockpile

machinery. Not to forge new fields of vision
        or technological accomplishment,
    no, merely to maintain the state

that we and our ancestors had grown
        accustomed to assume
    was civilization.

Let me tell it to you straight: a man in a highbacked chair
      will stop at nothing
    to grind you to dust

so you'd better put some metal in the mix
      to foil the sifters.
    I know whereof I speak.

I was there at the concrete parade.
      I threw bottles with the martyrs.
    I believed in the slogans I was shouting.

And if now I huddle in my hovel
      with not a name to my name
    think not that it's been some punishment

for my sins but merely the natural consequence
      of saying No
    to those who only hear Hooyah.

I am ruined but defiant, and my kidneys
      pucker from cleansing
    my blood of all that bile.

But I will achieve solace when the next cohort
      rises to bring forth
    a new era of idealism.

I await you, dear rampagers,
      at the junction of faith,
    rage, and frustration,

with my flag loosely furled
    and a chemical formula
    that will surprise you with its potency.

Come forth, angry children.
        Release me from my despair.
    I stand ready with my slouch,

my crooked shoulder,
        and my angry bag of beans.

Girds Us with Might

...אוזר ישראל בגבורה.

I had planned
on growing old and damned

but curses came early
and first light,

half mist, half calorie,
can't break enough

to bristle. My Y sleeps
curled around the scars

on her heart. Every hour
new insults and miseries

are invented for mothers
to lob at each other

over fences.
The day begins

with another boil advisory
and a homemade hammer.

We Will Rebuild

The protesters were sedate at the cemetery
    leaning their signs on the ground
unlike last time when there was so much fun.

The bald preacher chanted lines from a holy
    script and sent us all to mourning —
before we'd only been angry and hollow,

now our feelings had transcended us. Someone
    sang an old hymn with hope
still nestled in it, like a bean seed in a milk jug.

But who were these men in bulging suits
    with earpieces and gold teeth?
Which organization did they represent?

Who received their signals? We were among
    the counted, there at the graveside,
as the unionized functionary pushed clean

sand onto our friend, who had not yet seen
    enough baseball, or misery, or skin.
Then we were encouraged to disperse.

We drove to Legoland because the kids had
    had their fill of talk
and needed injection-moulded plastic blocks

with smooth monochrome surfaces and uniform
    interlock to soothe them.
While they built a perfect civilization in the play

area I cobbled together a lopsided contraption
    that couldn't stand firm
against a passing slobbering toddler.

That Such As These Are in Your World

שׁכָּכָה לוֹ בְּעוֹלָמוֹ...

Just past dawn a brown woman

    strolls her beige baby

laughing through a mouthful

    of cream cheese

I will not refrain from praise

    the bright fat the white teeth

the child's feet clapping

    under her seat

I will not miss my chance

    launch what I hope

is a welcome Good Morning from the porch

    too loud for this hour

am I creepy or not

is this the best I can do

mother half smiles child

displays the bagel

Crowns Us with Glory

...עוטר ישראל בתפארה.

On the porch, the hoe
    and a bag of good dirt.

Smell of water on warm wood.

Sunrise and the busy sounds
    of creatures emerging into new light.

I lift my paper face to dawn's probing,
    worship of a kind even
        sparrows understand
who know nothing but the weight of their hungry wings.

After all this, Pale Sufferer, Chief Flunky,
    can we continue on good terms?

Y drifts from room to room
    in a new blue robe.

I yearn for her, her tentative walk down the stairs.

I can only be witness
    and nursemaid
        to my world's recovery.

Out in the neighbourhood a city
    bus pulls through its route
        with purpose and a smoky cough.

I will praise as I must
    before the day heaves to its feet

here in my house
    not quite forsaken.

Gives Strength to the Weary

...הנותן ליעף כוח.

After the massacre
    we gather at dawn
to build a ring around
    the mosque while
the forensics fellows
    continue their insect
inspection. Last night we faced in
    trying to understand
but this morning we look
    up and away
summoning You
    the Unresponsible.
Some sad Sunday
    commuters slow
as they roll past
    on their way
to a new day.
    Back home
Y is drinking milky
    decaf on the porch.
Time to get back to work.
    Let these prayers
gird me for what's still looming.

Removes Sleep from the Eyelids

הַמַּעֲבִיר שֵׁינָה מֵעֵינַי וּתְנוּמָה מֵעַפְעַפָּי...

A good soaking overnight
and now the clouds
hover spent, going nowhere.
Already the yellow jackets
are up looking for someone
to mess with. Blue jays
mock my prayer which
would be fine if only
they'd help clear last night's
plates and tissues. But no,
they had no part in the mess
and they won't help
with the aftermath.
My Y is busy recomposing
herself from shining fragments
and my boys are off
to learn about the world.
Something just fell out of a tree.
Don't say I was fooled
into thinking I could matter.
Say rather . . . Say instead,
say nevertheless. Say even still.

Acknowledgements

I am indebted to Rabbi Lawrence A. Hoffman, whose Volume 5 of *My People's Prayerbook* on the *Birkhot HaShachar* informed my thinking about these prayers.

Thanks to the following publications who published earlier versions of these poems:

Allium, Arkansas International, Fiddlehead, Humber Literary Review, Literary Review of Canada, Michigan Quarterly Review, NewPoetry.ca, Reform Jewish Quarterly, Shirim, Vallum, and *The Walrus.*

An earlier version of "Emptying the Drains" was included in *Another Dysfunctional Cancer Poem Anthology*, edited by Priscila Uppal (z"l) and Meaghan Strimas (Mansfield Press, 2018). Thanks to everyone involved in that remarkable anthology.

An earlier version of "Whale Fall Suspension" was published in *Watch Your Head: Writers & Artists Respond to the Climate Crisis*, edited by Kathryn Mockler (Coach House, 2020). That one's good, too; go get it.

For empathetic early readers, heartfelt thanks to David O'Meara, Dionne Brand, David Goldstein, Vivé Griffith, Phil Metres, Jacob McArthur Mooney, Vivé again.

Thanks again to the good people at ECW, who are making a publishing home for me with humour, spunk, and grace, especially Michael Holmes, Jack David, David Caron, Shannon Parr, Jessica Albert, Jen Albert, Rachel Ironstone for the fabulous cover, and Emily Schultz for her vigilant eye. Also thanks to Cy Strom for taking such care with the Hebrew.

Loving thanks to Yael for giving me permission to write about private material.